According to God

...You are Absolutely Wonderful!

A Faith-Based Guide to Healing & Self-Care

Amy Seligson, LPC

According to God…You are Absolutely Wonderful!
ISBN 979-8-218-43482-3
eBook ISBN 979-8-218-43481-6

Published by:
SUNRISE PUBLISHING GROUP LLC
Brunswick, Georgia
info@sunrisepublishinggroup.com

Illustrated by Beth Snider, *BethSniderArt.com*
Design by Monica Thomas for TLC Book Design, *TLCBookDesign.com*
Proofread by Anne Campbell

Disclaimer: The information in this book is not intended to diagnose or treat any particular disease and/or condition. Nothing contained herein is meant to replace qualified medical or psychological advice and/or services. The author and publisher do not assume responsibility for how the reader chooses to apply the techniques herein. Use of the information is at the reader's discretion and discernment. The author and publisher specifically disclaim any and all liability arising directly or indirectly from the use or application of content contained in this book.

Nothing contained in this book is to be considered medical advice for any specific situation. This information is not intended as a substitute for the advice or medical care of a physician prior to taking any personal action with respect to the information contained in this book. This book and all of its contents are intended for educational and informational purposes only. The information in this book is believed to be reliable, but is presented without guaranty or warranty.

By reading further, you agree to release the author and publisher from any damages or injury associated with your use of the material in this book.

Contents

God thinks you are amazing!

Place
a photo
of yourself
here.

This book is dedicated
to Terri Wagner

Introduction

Hello dear reader! Yay! I am so glad that you have found this book and that you are reading it! You are truly wonderful, according to God. He adores you so much and wants you to know that! But to be honest, sometimes this can be hard to believe, especially when life goes sideways. That is why this book is jam-packed with God's Word and cool ways to learn more about Him and yourself. It can serve as a reminder of who you really are in the Lord and that you are SO wonderful!

This is *your* time to be free and honest with yourself and God. There are no expectations, pressure, or right and wrong answers with this book. You can color, draw, write, get silly, and get creative in it. You can be exactly who God created you to be in this safe space.

My prayer is that you may use this tool to gain greater insight into yourself as you take this crazy adventure called life with the Lord, Himself…and that you have a ton of fun while doing so! Just let loose and get creative with God!

Respectfully,

Amy Seligson, LPC

Who am I?

I am who GOD says I am

> *Before I formed you in the womb I knew you,*
> *before you were born I set you apart;*
> *I appointed you as a prophet to the nations.*
>
> **Jeremiah 1:5**

Read that again! You are who God says you are! Sometimes, you are not who you say you are. You are not always who you think you are. Why, might you ask? Because sometimes our thoughts and feelings can lie to us. We don't have to believe everything we think and feel. As a therapist, I hear so many people say what they don't like about themselves. But when I ask them to make lists and identity things that they like and love about themselves, they seem to struggle. It is truly heartbreaking to see how many people really don't like themselves at all! This type of thinking serves no good and only digs us further into a hole. We need to start looking at ourselves in a way that God does: in a loving and kind way.

How does GOD see you?

I praise you because I am fearfully and wonderfully made;
your works are wonderful, I know that full well.

Psalm 139:14

The LORD appeared to us in the past, saying: "I have loved you with an
everlasting love; I have drawn you with unfailing kindness."

Jeremiah 31:3

They will wage war against the Lamb, but the Lamb will triumph over
them because he is Lord of lords and King of kings — and with
him will be his called, chosen and faithful followers.

Revelation 17:14

And the God of all grace, who called you to his eternal glory in Christ,
after you have suffered a little while, will himself restore you and
make you strong, firm and steadfast.

1 Peter 5:10

"For I know the plans I have for you," declares the LORD, "plans to prosper
you and not to harm you, plans to give you hope and a future."

Jeremiah 29:11

According to God…You Are Absolutely Wonderful!

I *am* beautiful

Believe it because it is true! As humans, it is so easy to get caught up in our appearances and feel like we are not enough or maybe that we are too much. We catch ourselves comparing, contrasting, or wishing we looked a different way, starting with our hair and going all the way to our feet. We tend to be critical and we emotionally beat ourselves up...and for what? Just to feel crappier about ourselves which, by the way, is not a helpful solution. It seems like the more we focus on the negative aspects of our physical appearances, the more our moods plummet. Instead of focusing on the negatives, let's look at the positives. What is it that you like or maybe and hopefully **love** about your body? Draw a picture of yourself below and write what makes *you* beautiful on it.

☞ And now it is your turn

Yes, that is right. It is your turn to make a list of 10 positive things that you *like* about yourself and 10 things that you *love* about yourself. I know that this can be hard, awkward, weird or _____ (*fill in the blank with whatever you may be feeling right now*). It might feel unnatural for you to make this list, but it is important to recognize and own the positive qualities that you have. Sometimes our negative self-talk can be so hurtful that we would never say these things to somebody else. So, if it is that bad, why is it okay to say it to ourselves? Well, here's the truth, **it's not okay to talk to ourselves like that**. Many times, our negative self-talk just gets us further into trouble and does not help anything. This is a chance to change that, to shift your focus from the negative to the positive. You will notice that the first 3 sentences below start with the word "I." Instead of only writing down your strengths, I would like you to write "I" and then your strength each time. Using the word "I" personalizes the strength as you take ownership of it. After the third sentence, you will have to write your own "I" each time, but I thought you might need help with the first few as this can be difficult.

◄ 10 things I **LIKE** about myself ►

I ....

I ....

I ....

....

....

....

....

According to God…You Are Absolutely Wonderful!

....

....

....

10 things I LOVE about myself

I ....

I ....

I ....

....

....

....

....

....

Journal prompts about who you are

1. How do I see myself?

2. Is how I see myself helpful or hurtful for me?

3. When did I start seeing myself that way?

4. How do I think others see me?

Prayer requests

Write or draw your prayer requests about your identity.

According to God...You Are Absolutely Wonderful!

 # Praise reports

Write or draw your praise reports about your identity.

Study Two

The Power of Our Thoughts

The power to harm or the power to heal

We demolish arguments and every pretension that sets itself up against the knowledge of God, and we take captive every thought to make it obedient to Christ.

2 Corinthians 10:5

The Bible has been around much longer than the study of psychology has. It is interesting as a Christian when there are psychological theories that the world has come up with that align with what the Bible says. Psychology is finally getting caught up to the Bible in some ways. There are theories in psychology that focus on the importance of healthy thinking patterns. Research has shown that our behaviors, words, and emotions can all be significantly impacted by what and how we think. Science is proving what the Bible says about our thoughts. For centuries, the Bible has encouraged people to take control of their thoughts and focus on God and what is good. Psychologists have found that if we focus on negativity, then our emotions will decline. God's Word has been saying that much longer than the mental health field has. This helps show that God's Word is true.

What does GOD say about thoughts?

Set your minds on things above, not on earthly things.

Colossians 3:2

*Do not conform to the pattern of this world, but be transformed
by the renewing of your mind. Then you will be able to test and approve
what God's will is — his good, pleasing and perfect will.*

Romans 12:2

*Finally, brothers and sisters, whatever is true, whatever is noble,
whatever is right, whatever is pure, whatever is lovely, whatever is admirable —
if anything is excellent or praiseworthy — think about such things.*

Philippians 4:8

The simple believe anything, but the prudent give thought to their steps.

Proverbs 14:15

According to God...You Are Absolutely Wonderful!

☞ What to do with our positive and negative thoughts

Sometimes our thoughts are like garbage, and they just need to be removed from our lives because they are gross and toxic. Other thoughts need to be recognized and acknowledged every day, like special portraits on a wall. First, write your negative thoughts above the trash can, because they are hurtful. Next, write your positive thoughts in the picture frame and try to think about them and acknowledge them every day, because they are helpful.

Journal prompts about your thoughts

1. What are some thoughts that I have about myself that are hurting me?

2. Where did those thoughts come from and when did they start?

According to God…You Are Absolutely Wonderful!

3. Are these thoughts serving me in healthy ways?

4. What is one thing that I can do differently each day to help make my thoughts be more positive?

 # Prayer requests

Write or draw your prayer requests about your thoughts.

According to God...You Are Absolutely Wonderful!

 # Praise reports

Write or draw your praise reports about your thoughts.

Study Three
Depression

And we know that in all things God works for the good of those who love him, who have been called according to his purpose.

Romans 8:28

Depression is a big word. Depression is something that we have been exposed to one way or the other by either experiencing it personally or by knowing a person who has gone through this storm. The root word for depression is "pressed down." The phrase "pressed down" is a very illustrative way to describe depression. Depression can feel like being pushed down into a dark black hole with seemingly no light or hope to provide ease or comfort. Depression may be lonely and cold as in a perceived bottomless pit. As counterintuitive as this may seem, super cool stuff can happen when something is pressed down. For example, looking at the natural world, an acorn was once pressed down in the darkness of the cold, damp soil without the light of day. However, in due time the seedling, after being pressed down, begins to grow by cropping out of the ground. As the tree takes in water, sunlight, and food from the soil, it matures into a full tree that can bear fruit. When the tree bears fruit, the fruit helps people around it as it provides sustenance. God does not waste any experience that we go through. God puts things in our lives that will help us and others move closer to Him. God will use the depression that you are experiencing for His greater good.

What does GOD'S WORD say about depression?

The LORD is close to the brokenhearted
and saves those who are crushed in spirit.

Psalm 34:18

Come to me, all you who are weary and burdened, and I will give you rest.
Take my yoke upon you and learn from me, for I am gentle and humble in heart,
and you will find rest for your souls. For my yoke is easy and my burden is light.

Matthew 11:28–30

Hear my cry, O God; listen to my prayer. From the ends of the earth I call to you,
I call as my heart grows faint; lead me to the rock that is higher than I.
For you have been my refuge, a strong tower against the foe. I long to dwell
in your tent forever and take refuge in the shelter of your wings.

Psalm 61:1–4

According to God...You Are Absolutely Wonderful!

 # Draw a picture

Draw a picture of your tree and the "fruit" that you have or will produce.

Journal prompts about depression

1. What resonated with me on the topic of depression?

2. In what areas of my life do I feel pressed down?

According to God...You Are Absolutely Wonderful!

3. Does depression run in my family? If so, who else struggles with depression?

4. When I am feeling depressed, what are healthy coping skills that I can use to feel better?

 # Prayer requests

Write or draw your prayer requests about depression.

According to God…You Are Absolutely Wonderful!

 # Praise reports

Write or draw your praise reports about depression.

Study Four

Worry & Anxiety

Do not be anxious about anything, but in every situation, by prayer and petition, with thanksgiving, present your requests to God. And the peace of God, which transcends all understanding, will guard your hearts and your minds in Christ Jesus.

Philippians 4: 6–7

The root word for worry means "to strangle." Meanwhile, the word anxiety comes from "troubled in mind" and "constricted" or "tight." Don't those meanings just hit the bullseye on the target? Anxiety can be a similar feeling as if we were getting physically strangled, which can sometimes feel like we are dying. Worry and anxiety can choke us with fear, leaving us under an enormous amount of pressure and the feelings that we can't escape. But God! God can use this scary, lonely, constricting place of anxiety and worry to produce beautiful treasures not only in yourself but in others, too! If we look at the physical world, we can see that in order to produce a diamond, there needs to be a significant amount of heat and constrictive pressure. God can use that place of pressure, strangle, fear, mental constriction, and troubled mind to produce something brilliant in you that you had no idea existed. You may realize that you are stronger, braver, and more capable than you ever thought you could be. For example, you may have more empathy and humility, having experienced the anxiety. God does not waste anything and that includes feelings of worry and anxiety.

What does GOD say about worry and anxiety?

The LORD himself goes before you and will be with you;
he will never leave you nor forsake you.
Do not be afraid; do not be discouraged.

Deuteronomy 31:8

I have told you these things, so that in me you may have peace.
In this world you will have trouble. But take heart!
I have overcome the world.

John 16:33

Can any one of you by worrying add a single hour to your life?

Matthew 6:27

Then Jesus said to his disciples: "Therefore I tell you, do not worry about
your life, what you will eat; or about your body, what you will wear.
For life is more than food, and the body is more than clothes."

Luke 12:22–23

Cast all your anxiety on him because he cares for you.

1 Peter 5:7

According to God…You Are Absolutely Wonderful!

⛰ Shine like the diamond you are!

Write about or draw a picture of what "diamonds" formed from the anxiety you experienced. Also, diamonds can be cut into smaller pieces and given to many different people. How have you given your "diamonds" away to help other people?

Journal prompts about worry & anxiety

1. When is anxiety triggered for me?

2. What parts of my body are affected by worry and anxiety?

According to God...You Are Absolutely Wonderful!

3. What thoughts do I have when I am feeling worried or anxious?

4. How can I help myself calm down from anxiety?

Prayer requests

Write or draw your prayer requests about worry and anxiety.

According to God...You Are Absolutely Wonderful!

 # Praise reports

Write or draw your praise reports about worry and anxiety.

Study Five

Who is Really in Control?

> *The LORD Almighty has sworn, "Surely, as I have planned,*
> *so it will be, and as I have purposed, so it will happen."*
>
> **Isaiah 14:24**

Life can get so crazy that sometimes the only thing that we feel we have control over is the remote and sometimes we don't even have control over that. As humans, we really, *really* want to be in control over everything, which (I know is hard to admit but) does include trying to control God. However, we are only in control of ourselves, which is a good thing. With God's help, we can have control over our thoughts, actions, words, and emotions. We do not have to fall victim to being controlled by outside factors such as people or events. We can choose to be kind and loving even if people aren't treating us the same way. We have the option to show respect even if it is not being reciprocated. We can choose to walk away instead of being sucked into toxic situations that could lead to negative decisions. We don't have to fall victim to factors outside of ourselves. People will do what they are going to do, but you still have the power to control yourself and not let the outside factors affect your joy and peace that God has given you.

Even though God has given self-control, He has the ultimate control over everything. There is no need to lose sleep because He has our backs. Jesus was definitely not losing sleep over anything. He made that quite clear in Matthew chapter 8 when He was in the boat with the disciples and a storm rolled in and yes, He was just snoozing away. Maybe we need to take our cues from Jesus, who does in fact have everything in His hands, including us. So, rest easy knowing that.

What does GOD say about God being in control?

Many are the plans in a person's heart, but it is the LORD's purpose that prevails.

Proverbs 19:21

In their hearts humans plan their course, but the LORD establishes their steps.

Proverbs 16:9

"For I know the plans I have for you," declares the LORD, "plans to prosper you and not to harm you, plans to give you hope and a future.

Jeremiah 29:11

Our God is in heaven; he does whatever pleases him.

Psalm 115:3

According to God…You Are Absolutely Wonderful!

🏔 Put it in God's hands

Draw or write what you are trying to control and put in God's hands…where it belongs.

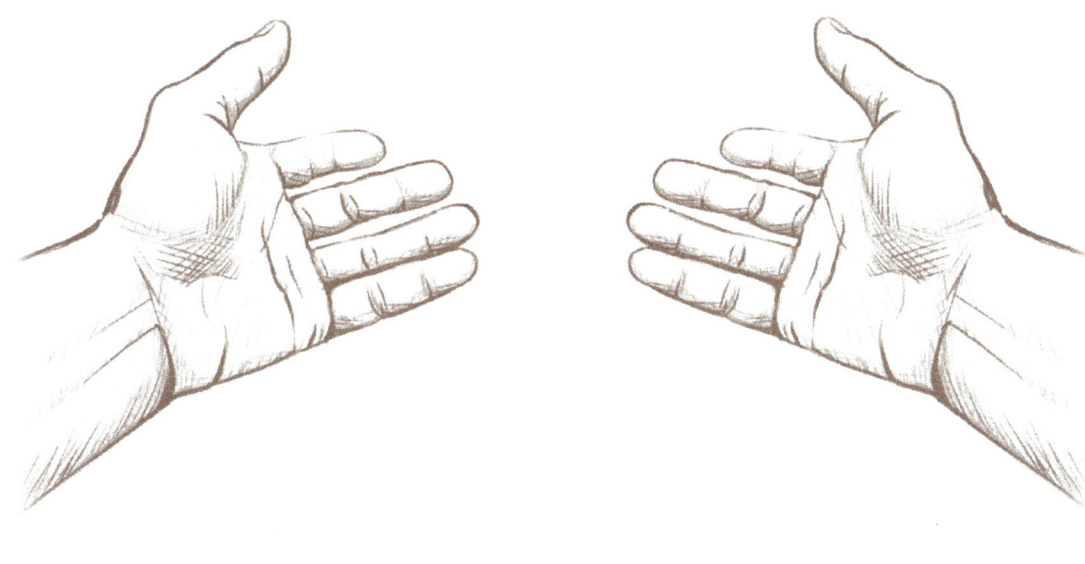

Journal prompts about control

1. Currently in my life, what am I trying to control?

2. What are my motivations for controlling these things?

According to God ... You Are Absolutely Wonderful!

3. Is trying to control these things hurting myself or others?

4. How can I give the desire to control things over to God?

Prayer requests

Write or draw your prayer requests about control.

According to God...You Are Absolutely Wonderful!

 # Praise reports

Write or draw your praise reports about control.

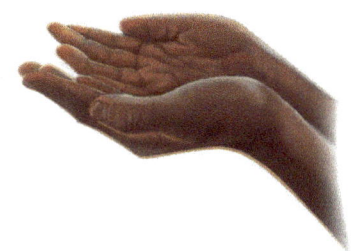

Study Six

Trauma

The LORD is a refuge for the oppressed,
a stronghold in times of trouble.

Psalm 9:9

The root word for trauma is "wound." The word "wound" is an excellent way to paint a picture of trauma. When hearing this word, you might think of a physical wound somewhere on a body. Although you may not see the damage of psychological trauma on a physical level, trauma very much lives in the body. You are *not* alone. God sees you, hears you, and is walking with you in this pain. God can also work through mental health and medical professionals to assist you in the healing process. You would not leave a physical wound open, bleeding and susceptible to infection, so why not tend to the psychological trauma wound? Not addressing a trauma can lead to possible mental health complications in the future. Like any fresh injury, it may hurt to clean it and put bandages on it but if you ignore the wound, it can hurt so much more.

What does GOD say about trauma?

*Trust in the LORD with all your heart and lean not on your own understanding;
in all your ways submit to him, and he will make your paths straight.*

Proverbs 3:5–6

I can do all this through him who gives me strength.

Philippians 4:13

*I waited patiently for the LORD; he turned to me and heard my cry.
He lifted me out of the slimy pit, out of the mud and mire;
he set my feet on a rock and gave me a firm place to stand.*

Psalm 40:1–2

According to God…You Are Absolutely Wonderful!

 # What wounds in your life need tending to?

Write or draw in the heart what comes up for you when thinking about trauma.

🌿 Journal prompts about trauma

1. Do I identify with having experienced trauma?

2. How have I coped with trauma so far?

3. Is the trauma affecting my life in any way?

4. How can I heal from the trauma?

 # Prayer requests

Write or draw your prayer requests about trauma.

According to God...You Are Absolutely Wonderful!

 # Praise reports

Write or draw your praise reports about trauma.

Study Seven

Anger

Fools give full vent to their rage,
but the wise bring calm in the end.

Proverbs 29:11

Anger hurts. Anger mostly hurts the person who is feeling this emotion. There may be times when we are so mad at someone, even though that person is not even aware that we are feeling this way. Or the individual might just not care that we are angry and hurting. Anger can keep a person up at night while the other person who the anger is directed towards could be just dreaming away without a care in the world. Anger is hurting the person feeling the anger, not the other way around. Anger can serve a purpose, but it does have the potential to harm as well. Sometimes we must dig a little deeper to get a better understanding of where this feeling is coming from. Anger is a primary emotion with other emotions underneath. The emotion anger may be masking other emotions such as hurt, pain, mistrust, betrayal, frustration, and even hunger. It is important to dive deeper into anger so that we can get at the root and remove it because, as God's Word says, anger can be destructive in our lives.

What does GOD say about anger?

*"In your anger do not sin": Do not let the sun go down
while you are still angry, and do not give the devil a foothold.*
Ephesians 4:26–27

*My dear brothers and sisters, take note of this: Everyone should be quick to listen,
slow to speak and slow to become angry, because human anger
does not produce the righteousness that God desires.*
James 1:19–20

A person's wisdom yields patience; it is to one's glory to overlook an offense.
Proverbs 19:11

Do not be quickly provoked in your spirit, for anger resides in the lap of fools.
Ecclesiastes 7:9

*Do not make friends with a hot-tempered person, do not associate with one
easily angered, or you may learn their ways and get yourself ensnared.*
Proverbs 22:24–25

According to God...You Are Absolutely Wonderful!

 Anger – digging deeper

Draw a picture of a weed (which depicts anger). Next, draw a picture of a root system or seed that represents the other emotions the anger is connected to. What are the other feelings underneath the anger and where did the seed of this weed (that is, anger) come from?

Journal prompts about anger

1. When do I notice myself getting angry?

2. Is there a pattern to when I feel angry with myself, other people, or situations?

According to God...You Are Absolutely Wonderful!

3. How is anger negatively impacting me? Other people?

4. How can I cope with anger in healthy ways?

 # Prayer requests

Write or draw your prayer requests about anger.

According to God...You Are Absolutely Wonderful!

 # Praise reports

Write or draw your praise reports about anger.

Study Eight
Forgiveness

> *Be kind and compassionate to one another, forgiving each other,*
> *just as in Christ God forgave you.*
>
> **Ephesians 4:32**

Imagine sitting in a cold, dark, and lonely prison cell. This cell has robbed you from enjoying yourself and those around you to the greatest degree. The God-given potential within yourself is limited and you are not able to soar high above the clouds as you are just sitting in the confines of jail. But what if someone walked up and handed you the keys to get out of this miserable jail sentence? The keys that will lead you to freedom, joy, peace, and even happiness. Would you dare to open the door and choose to free yourself from the torment or would you choose to continue to live your days out in bondage and suffering? Unforgiveness is bondage. Unforgiveness is prison. Unforgiveness is miserable. Unforgiveness steals from us, but unforgiveness does not necessarily rob or steal from the people who we do not forgive. Mostly, it just steals from us, perpetually.

Let's be real, forgiving people is not always easy. Forgiveness normally takes work. Choosing forgiveness is an intentional process of dismissing a person from their choices without any residual ill-will towards them. Forgiveness does not justify or make their choices acceptable, but it does allow you to be free from bondage, by not holding resentment and bitterness towards someone.

Who do you need to forgive? Do you need to forgive God? Other people? Yourself? Will you choose to take the key to forgiveness and free yourself from the prison you are in?

When you are thinking about who you need to forgive, you might want to think about who needs to forgive you and for what.

What does GOD say about forgiveness?

*'And forgive us our debts, as we also have forgiven our debtors.
And lead us not into temptation, but deliver us from the evil one.' For if you forgive
other people when they sin against you, your heavenly Father will also forgive you.*

Matthew 6:12–14

*Bear with each other and forgive one another if any of you has
a grievance against someone. Forgive as the Lord forgave you.*

Colossians 3:13

*Then Peter came to Jesus and asked, "Lord, how many times shall I forgive
my brother or sister who sins against me? Up to seven times?" Jesus answered,
"I tell you, not seven times, but seventy-seven times."*

Matthew 18:21–22

According to God…You Are Absolutely Wonderful!

 # What is stopping you from being free?

Write or draw what your life would look like if you were free from unforgiveness.

Journal prompts about forgiveness

1. Did reading about forgiveness stir up any emotions and/or thoughts inside me?

2. How is holding onto unforgiveness serving me?

According to God…You Are Absolutely Wonderful!

3. Is there anything in my life that I think is unforgivable?

4. What would my life look like if I did forgive?

 # Prayer requests

Write or draw your prayer requests about forgiveness.

 # Praise reports

Write or draw your praise reports about forgiveness.

Study Nine

Gratitude

Give thanks in all circumstances;
for this is God's will for you in Christ Jesus.

1 Thessalonians 5:18

Years ago, I heard a professor refer to the 90/10 rule as when 90 percent of our lives are going well and 10 percent of our lives are going bad, we tend to focus only on the 10 percent that is bad. Does the 90/10 rule speak to you? Sometimes, we may get so caught up in the little parts that go wrong that we fail to see and enjoy all the blessings that God has bestowed upon us. Gratitude is a game changer! This is another situation where science has finally caught up with the Word of God! The Bible has been talking about the importance of gratitude for centuries and now science has shown that practicing gratitude does make a positive impact on our thoughts and emotions. Gratitude can shift our perspectives from what is lacking to seeing all the blessings that God has given us!

What does GOD say about gratitude?

Let the peace of Christ rule in your hearts, since as members of one body you were called to peace. And be thankful. Let the message of Christ dwell among you richly as you teach and admonish one another with all wisdom through psalms, hymns, and songs from the Spirit, singing to God with gratitude in your hearts. And whatever you do, whether in word or deed, do it all in the name of the Lord Jesus, giving thanks to God the Father through him.

Colossians 3:15–17

Give thanks to the LORD, for he is good; his love endures forever.

Psalm 118:29

Enter his gates with thanksgiving and his courts with praise; give thanks to him and praise his name.

Psalm 100:4

According to God...You Are Absolutely Wonderful!

☞ What am I thankful for?

You can write or draw what you are thankful for. There are no right or wrong answers.

I am thankful for ....

I am thankful for ....

I am thankful for ....

I ....

I ....

I ....

Journal prompts about gratitude

1. What do I take for granted in my life?

2. How can I practice gratitude every day?

According to God...You Are Absolutely Wonderful!

3. How can I show gratitude towards others?

4. How can I show gratitude towards God?

 # Prayer requests

Write or draw your prayer requests about gratitude.

According to God...You Are Absolutely Wonderful!

 # Praise reports

Write or draw your praise reports about gratitude.

Study Ten
Get That Helper's High!

Win-win situation for the win! How can you go wrong with anything when everybody wins? You really can't go wrong. Everyone tends to win when we volunteer or give back. Science has demonstrated that there is such a thing as a helper's high. A helper's high is when the helper feels good while helping. It is super easy to get sucked into our own issues, but helping allows us to step outside of ourselves and our situations to positively impact the lives of others. Volunteering can assist in transferring the focus from us to others in need. Sometimes focusing on our own problems and shortcomings can create a negative head space. Helping allows us to be able to focus on a greater good and feel like we are part of a bigger plan. As God's kids, we are abundantly blessed. As our good Father gives freely to us, we can be Christ-like and give to others, also. At the end of the day, we absolutely cannot outgive God.

What does GOD say about helping and giving back?

*Give to everyone who asks you, and if anyone takes
what belongs to you, do not demand it back.*

Luke 6:30

Do not withhold good from those to whom it is due, when it is in your power to act.

Proverbs 3:27

*Therefore, as we have opportunity, let us do good to all people,
especially to those who belong to the family of believers.*

Galatians 6:10

My command is this: Love each other as I have loved you.

John 15:12

According to God...You Are Absolutely Wonderful!

☞ How can you give back? Let's get creative.

What are 3 ways you can give back with your time, money, and God-given talents?

Journal prompts about giving back

1. From what areas of my life can I give back?

2. Is it hard for me to give? If so, why?

3. What does giving back look like for me?

4. How do I feel when I give back?

 **Prayer requests**

Write or draw your prayer requests about giving back.

According to God...You Are Absolutely Wonderful!

 # Praise reports

Write or draw your praise reports about giving back.

Study Eleven

Take Care of Yourself...Really!

By the seventh day God had finished the work he had been doing; so on the seventh day he rested from all his work.

Genesis 2:2

Self-care is one of those aspects in life that does not seem super important until we are completely exhausted or even burnt out. It might sound strange but self-care can sometimes be like balancing a checkbook. To keep a healthy bank account, deposits must be made in order to replenish what has been withdrawn. If there are too many withdrawals and not enough deposits, the account will be overdrafted with outrageous fees that nobody wants to pay. If finances are really out of balance, then bankruptcy can happen. We pay similar prices emotionally, mentally, physically, and even spiritually when we don't balance ourselves, as well. Giving to others when you don't have anything to give can lead to overdrafts with big fees. When we give, we are making withdrawals from our emotional, mental, physical, and spiritual bank accounts. It is okay to make withdrawals from those "bank accounts" because that is why they are there. However, a problem happens when we do not put deposits in the form of self-care back, which can lead to frustration, exhaustion, and burnout. When we become overdrawn or even emotionally bankrupt, we can not be the best for ourselves or the others around us. We must stay balanced and care for ourselves so we can show Christ to the world and do what God has called us to do.

What does GOD say about self-care?

*Very early in the morning, while it was still dark, Jesus got up,
left the house and went off to a solitary place, where he prayed.*

Mark 1:35

*Come to me, all you who are weary and burdened, and I will give you rest. Take my
yoke upon you and learn from me, for I am gentle and humble in heart, and you will
find rest for your souls. For my yoke is easy and my burden is light.*

Matthew 11:28–30

*Then, because so many people were coming and going that they did not even
have a chance to eat, he said to them, "Come with me by yourselves
to a quiet place and get some rest."*

Mark 6:31

*In vain you rise early and stay up late, toiling for food to eat —
for he grants sleep to those he loves.*

Psalm 127:2

According to God…You Are Absolutely Wonderful!

☞ Self-care list → Self-care life

There are many different forms of self-care. You can give yourself care physically, emotionally, spiritually, and mentally. What are some ways that you can take care of yourself? There are some examples here, but you can fill in the rest because you know yourself the best. Please remember to fill out the "When" section because it is important to be intentional with your time.

I can read the Bible every day. .... **When:** in the morning for 15 minutes ....

I will go for a hike. .... **When:** Tuesday at 5:30 pm after work for 1 hour

I will take a bath. .... **When:** Saturday morning ....

I .... **When:** ....

I .... **When:** ....

I .... **When:** ....

I .... **When:** ....

I .... **When:** ....

I .... **When:** ....

I .... **When:** ....

I .... **When:** ....

I .... **When:** ....

I .... **When:** ....

I .... **When:** ....

I .... **When:** ....

Journal prompts about self-care

1. What is preventing me from exercising self-care?

2. Do I experience guilt for taking care of myself? Why or why not?

According to God...You Are Absolutely Wonderful!

3. What self-care strategies did I do in the past and do not do now?

4. Has self-care helped me in the past? If so, how did it help me?

 # Prayer requests

Write or draw your prayer requests about self-care.

According to God...You Are Absolutely Wonderful!

 # Praise reports

Write or draw your praise reports about self-care.

Study Twelve
Bust-A-Move!

> *As the body without the spirit is dead,*
> *so faith without deeds is dead.*
>
> **James 2:26**

Alright! Well, the time has come in this journal between yourself and God for you to make a plan. As Christians, we need to take action. Do something! Everybody's something will look okay because God does not have the same exact plan for everybody...whew...that's a good thing because how boring would that be if we all had the same lives?

How are you going to get to where God wants you to be? Thinking about the next steps can be super overwhelming. When tasks are daunting, chunking them out into smaller pieces can take off a lot of pressure. Instead of looking at a year from now, let's split it up into pieces and look at the next month. Where do you want to be in one month? Once you've figured that out, move to 3 months, then 6 months, then 12 months, and then 2 years.

What does GOD say about planning?

In their hearts humans plan their course, but the LORD establishes their steps.

Proverbs 16:9

May he give you the desire of your heart and make all your plans succeed.

Psalm 20:4

Many are the plans in a person's heart, but it is the LORD's purpose that prevails.

Proverbs 19:21

Let the morning bring me word of your unfailing love, for I have put my trust in you.
Show me the way I should go, for to you I entrust my life.

Psalm 143:8

According to God...You Are Absolutely Wonderful!

1 month BUST-A-MOVE plan

3 month BUST-A-MOVE plan

According to God...You Are Absolutely Wonderful!

6 month BUST-A-MOVE plan

12 month BUST-A-MOVE plan

According to God...You Are Absolutely Wonderful!

2 year BUST-A-MOVE plan

Journal prompts about my bust-a-move plans

1. What can I do to help these plans be successful?

2. What are potential barriers to my plans?

According to God...You Are Absolutely Wonderful!

3. What is my Plan B if the original plans don't work? (It is okay to have a Plan C or D, too).

4. How will I celebrate when my plans succeed?

Prayer requests

Write or draw prayer requests about your bust-a-move plans.

According to God...You Are Absolutely Wonderful!

 # Praise reports

Write or draw your praise reports about your bust-a-move plans.

Closing Prayer

Dear Lord,

I come before You to thank You for readers like _____ *(fill the blank in with your name)* who is reading this prayer.

Jesus, I may not know them, but You do. You know them more than they know themselves. You knew them when You knitted them in their mothers' wombs, and You know how many hairs are on their heads right now. You not only know them, but You love them beyond measure as they are Your beloved children. I pray that they know You and love You, too! They are not reading this by accident or by coincidence. You have them here for a reason and You have **BIG** plans for them. Your plans are to prosper them and to not hurt them. Thank You for bringing them this far and thank You for all of the things that You are doing in their lives. Jesus, please meet them where they are and let them know that You are with them every step of the way in this crazy adventure called life. I pray that they see You in ways that they have never seen You before and that their relationships with You grow. I pray that each person has peace beyond all understanding and that they know that You have come to give life and give life more abundantly. Lord, I want to pray for healing and blessings on each person reading this and please pour out blessings on their friends and families, as well. In Jesus' name I pray. Amen.

If you would like, you can add to this closing prayer, too...

www.ingramcontent.com/pod-product-compliance
Lightning Source LLC
Chambersburg PA
CBHW041145120626
46547CB00020B/3120